PRISONERS OF IMAGE

ETHNIC AND GENDER STEREOTYPES

Prisoners of Image
Ethnic and Gender Stereotypes

JANUARY 7—MARCH 4, 1989, ALTERNATIVE MUSEUM, NEW YORK CITY

PRISONERS OF IMAGE
ETHNIC AND GENDER
STEREOTYPES

Library of Congress Catalog
Card Number: 88-84137
©The Alternative Museum, 1989
17 White Street
New York, N.Y. 10013
Tel. (212) 966-4444

ISBN 932075-24-x
First Edition

The exhibition was supported
in part by public funds from
the Museum Program, New
York State Council on the
Arts.

Exhibiting Artists

Perry Bard
Terry Berkowitz
Robert Colescott
Anton Van Dalen
Bing Lee
Robin Michaels
Martha Rosler
Ben Sakoguchi
Coreen Simpson
Lorna Simpson
Tom of Finland
Carrie Mae Weems

Collections

The Balch Institute
for Ethnic Studies,
Philadelphia

The Janette Faulkner Collection
of Stereotypes and Caricature
of Afro-Americans,
San Francisco

The Cartoonist and Writers'
Syndicate Portfolio,
New York City

Essays

Robbin Legere Henderson
E. San Juan, Jr.
Jerry Robinson
Fawaz Turki
Judith Wilson

Curators

Robbin Legere Henderson
Geno Rodriguez

MAMMY BANK. Cast Iron. 1910 U.S.A. 5¾ x 3 x 1¾ inches.
From the Janette Faulkner Collection of Stereotypes and Caricature of Afro-Americans.

"These caricatures and stereotypes
were really intended as prisons. Prisons without the traditional bars, but
prisons of image. Inside each desperately grinning "sambo" and each placid three hundred pound "mammy"
lamp there is imprisoned a real person, someone we know. If you look
hard at the collection and don't panic
...you will begin to really see, the
eyes and then the hearts of these despised relatives of ours, who have
been forced to lock their spirits away
from themselves and away from
us...." Alice Walker

Alice Walker on the Janette Faulkner Collection

PRISONS OF IMAGE

BY ROBBIN LEGERE HENDERSON

This is not a collection of artifacts about black history. Most of the imagery in the collection was created by white people, and it serves as a rationale to ignore and even to condone injustice, discrimination, segregation and racism. In 1982 Janette Faulkner and I presented a large exhibition of items from her collection at the Berkeley Art Center in Berkeley, California. The exhibition was entitled "Ethnic Notions, Black Images in the White Mind." Our goal was to demonstrate how the past and continuing presence of such items serves to create and perpetuate damaging stereotypes, either consciously or unconsciously. By presenting these objects in historical and social perspective we hoped to promote an understanding of how stereotyping functions to promote racism and how items such as those displayed in the exhibition reinforce negative attitudes. Our intention was to provide an opportunity for people to reflect on the formation of ethnic attitudes and thereby to empower them to change.

Public response was strong and at times moving. On leaving the exhibition one woman remarked that the presentation of these objects had revealed to her how prejudicial attitudes with which she had always been uncomfortable had been internalized by the unremarkable presence of these items in kitchens, parlors and on lawns as she was growing up. She said that she had never understood why she had such deep feelings of fear and aversion to African Americans whom her intellect told her were her equals. Why had she held these uncomfortable and wrong feelings? Seeing the exhibition she began to understand that these feelings were not the result of some evil within her, but a result of subtle and insidious messages she had received growing up in Maine—imagery and verbal references from her environment long buried, but of course, periodically reinforced by imagery, words and actions which permeate our society. This material is nearly as damaging to the class which created it as it is to those it denigrates.

The mute presence of items such as these reinforce ethnic attitudes formed by other cultural influences: family, peers, media, films, songs and stories. All these influences are reinforced by contact with the others. Stereotype is an attempt to depersonalize individuals and thereby deny them the rights and dignity which our society professes to accord everyone. Although we have identified nine specific African American stereotypes prevalent in our society, they overlap, blend or contradict one another—stereotyping is not rational. In almost all cases physical distortion is used to accentuate the African American's "otherness." Along with the exaggeration of physical differences, African Americans have been stereotyped as behaving differently from whites, having only menial occupations, being primitives or natural victims. The black woman, when she is depicted here, is almost always a nurturing "mammy," the servant of whites. Children are "pickaninnies" or unnatural "golliwogs." In addition, certain symbols are recurrently associated with blacks: the watermelon, cotton, the "coon," the alligator, the chicken. The Black Entertainer overlaps with all of the above, adding the stereotype of the African American as the object of amusement for white audiences, while perpetuating the other stereotypes.

The distortion of black physical appearance is one way in which whites have attempted to distance themselves, socially, emotionally, intellectually and physically from blacks. Whites have historically promulgated myths about black physical (as well as intellectual and moral) inferiority. These myths had no basis in fact, of course, but spoke to a need in whites to rationalize enslavement, racism, segregation and discrimination. The exaggeratedly flat noses, the grinning, long white teeth surrounded by large red lips and the bulging, white rolling eyes are contemptuous depictions of black physical characteristics. These stereotypes have served to dehumanize black people and to reinforce the walls of separateness that whites have erected against full participation by blacks in American society.

White Americans have had difficulty reconciling American ideals of freedom and equality with the realities of slavery and racial discrimination. The argument that blacks were somewhat less than human served to justify white subordination of blacks. By defining blacks as savage, animalistic and sensual, whites could define themselves as everything blacks were not. This portrayal of blacks can be explained as a reflection of white people's insecurity about their own identities.

Among the most persistent black stereotypes is the image of the black woman whose sole purpose is to care for and comfort whites. She is often represented as a large, jolly, bandana-wearing person who tirelessly works for the benefit of her white "family." This image distorts the historical reality of black women. Slavery forced many black women to labor not only in the fields, but in white homes, kitchens and nurseries. These conditions often left black women with little time to care for their own families. This dual existence created considerable emotional turmoil for black women which belies the carefree, cheerful "Mammy" image that whites have promoted when depicting black women. The stereotype reflects the attempt by whites to limit the role of black women to caretakers and drudges, a gross distortion of the true attitudes black women had toward their work, their families and themselves.

Both slavery and the racial discrimination which has continued long after emancipation rest on a power relationship. The objects in this collection suggest ways in which the dominant society has viewed that relationship: blacks are pitiful, helpless and vulnerable whenever confronted with white power. Moreover, the objects trivialize racial oppression by suggesting that the brutal actions they depict are somehow humorous. Viewed within the context of racial violence—the widespread impulse among whites to brutalize blacks—it becomes painfully apparent why manufacturers assumed that there was a market for ashtrays and games which allowed whites to symbolically attack blacks, or golf tees which evoked images of "playful" sadism. The emotions and sensibilities expressed in these objects are identical to those which legitimize lynching and other forms of physical and psychological violence.

The people depicted in these objects display not the slightest impulse to resist; the targets usually are smiling, or helpless in their pain. As with much of this material in general, this represents wishful thinking and self-delusion on the part of the perpetrators. Blacks have resisted white brutality since they were first brought to our shores as slaves.

Black children have often been portrayed by whites as objects of humor and comic relief. The white stereotype has been that black children just "spring up" and flourish with little or no help from parents or other adults. Black children have been characterized as "mischievous," "carefree pickaninnies" forever getting in "trouble," but never really being in serious peril. In truth, however, black children have been subjected to brutality, labor at an early age and separation from their parents. Ignoring these realities, many whites have chosen to promote the "pickaninny" caricature of black childhood. Underlying the pickaninny image is a hostility toward black children which again serves to dehumanize them. The "Little African, a Dainty Morsel" item places a black child in a life-threatening situation that is depicted as "humorous." Compare this to the reality of the black children who faced white mobs as public schools were desegrated in the 1950s and 1960s. Black children have been further rendered sub-human by the monstrous caricature of the "Golliwog." These distorted grinning heads and grotesque faces of black children have been used to sell or identify household and other items. They are disturbing, distortions of black children's faces that have persisted through time.

Many whites have attempted to limit the role which blacks have played in American society by reducing black experiences to certain stereo-typed formulae. These symbols limit African Americans by falsely asserting that they are uncomplicated beings who are content with their subordinate position in society. Watermelon, chicken, cotton, the alligator and the "coon" have become symbolic of the black experience in the white mind.

Whites have put forth the myth that blacks' fondness for watermelon and chicken would drive them to any action—including stealing—to obtain these items. Cotton and the cotton field are other symbols by which whites have attempted to define blacks. The image of the "contented" blacks picking cotton is pervasive and enduring, although historically inaccurate.

In 1981 Alice Walker wrote:

"These caricatures and stereotypes were really intended as prisons. Prisons without the traditional bars, but prisons of image. Inside each desperately grinning "sambo" and each placid three hundred pound "mammy" lamp there is imprisoned a real person, someone we know. If you look hard at the collection and don't panic . . . you will begin to really see, the eyes and then the hearts of these despised relatives of ours, who have been forced to lock their spirits away from themselves and away from us. . . .

That is the way I now see Jan Faulkner's collection. I see our brothers and sisters, mothers and fathers, captured and forced into images they did not devise, doing hard time for all of us.

We can liberate them by understanding this. And free ourselves."

Little has happened in the nearly ten years since this was written to give assurance that any of us is closer to being liberated from these imprisoning depictions of ourselves and our brothers and sisters. Nevertheless, it is necessary that we continue to confront these images and the social conditions that allow them to endure. For only by identifying and challenging these ubiquitous caricatures and indeed all stereotypes can we liberate ourselves from a prison that threatens to isolate and dehumanize us all.

Robbin Legere Henderson is an artist and writer. She is also director of "China Books" in San Francisco.

CANDY. Paper and candy. 1981. Made in England this candy shows the persistence of the golliwog image. 9¼ x 2½ x ½ inches. From the Janette Faulkner Collection of Stereotypes and Caricature of Afro-Americans.

Top: CLEANING POWDER. Cardboard. Late 1920s early 1930s. This depicts "The Gold Dust Twins", an example of using the golliwog/ pickaninny image to sell a product. Originally the Fairbanks Brothers used their own portraits on the containers, but sales were slow. They improved when the "Twins" were substituted. The company was later taken over by Lever Brothers.
Below: BANK. Cast iron c. 1882. Known as the "Jolly Nigger" this bank was manufactured by the J.C. Stevens Company. The eyes roll when a coin is placed in the mouth and the lever on the shoulder is pressed. 6 x 5½ x 6 inches.
From the Janette Faulkner Collection of Stereotypes and Caricature of Afro-Americans.

Top: WINDUP TOYS. "Amos", 11½ x 4 x 2¼ inches. "Andy, 11¾ x 4 x 2⅞ inches. Louis Marx Company.
Below: TOOTHPASTE. Paper, metal and plastic. Currently manufactured by an English Company, a subsidiary of Palmolive Peet, Co., Hawley and Hazel, based in Taiwan. This toothpaste is marketed in Japan, Taiwan and the Middle East. 8 x 1⅞ x 1⅝ inches.
From the Janette Faulkner Collection of Stereotypes and Caricature of Afro-Americans.

Top: CIGAR BOX LABEL. Paper. c. 1910. 10 x 6 inches.
Below left: CUP HOLDER. Chalk, 1930, U.S.A. An example of the frequent use of the watermelon as a motif associated with Afro-Americans. 5 ¼ x 6 x 2 inches. Below right: GOLLIWOG PERFUME BOTTLES. Glass. 1910. Made by de Vigny Company, France. 6 x 4¼ x 3¼ inches. From the Janette Faulkner Collection of Stereotypes and Caricature of Afro-Americans.

VICTIMS OF THE LITERATURE OF POWER

BY FAWAZ TURKI

As the argument goes, Western culture has long since disavowed itself of its once-cherished fantasies concerning the "white man's burden." Moreover, it has witnessed racism's retreat and all its myths from the currency of rational exchange. The disorder that followed the collapse of Colonialism, which for so long had lumped together all non-whites simply as "other," gave rise to a new phraseology, a new tense, as it were, in the grammar of Western cultural perceptions.

The overwhelming majority of peoples once subjugated by a mere few, now found themselves autonomous. Westerners could no longer dismiss the Third World inhabitants as "niggers," "wogs" or "bicots". The mission cultural or mission civilatrice, a central issue in the white man's concept of his burden, ceased to serve and justify the objective realities imposed on colonized peoples.

After all, the argument continues, we no longer have pompous mediocrities such as Winston Churchill, epitomizing the racist, cold warrior, counter-revolutionary sentiments of an earlier age, dismissing the world's "wogs" with typical upperclass, British contempt, as did Churchill when he called Mahatma Gandhi "that mendicant ascending the stairs of the chancellery." We no longer have a French Foreign Office official insisting that the Tunisians could not be "granted" independence because they were not "ready" for it, or that the people of Chad could not be "trusted" with self-government because they "could not govern themselves."

English explorers no longer go to Africa and come back to tell their countrymen and other Europeans that they "discovered" Lake Victoria, even though the lake had long before been discovered, named, and its shores inhabited by native peoples. For forty years, Europeans have no longer gone to Africa to "interact" with Africans only to synthesize their experiences in books such as Born Free—books about animals that have rights presumably taking precedence over those of the native Africans amongst whom they had lived for decades and to whose aspirations they were obviously blind.

True, the decline of racist kitsch, fashionable less than half a century ago, is evident, not only in Western culture in general, but in American culture in particular, with the latter having experienced a civil rights movement of sorts that had organized social emotions into a coherent way for people to see one another. But the racist impulse has found more subterranean and belligerent channels of its expression.

In its most unencumbered and stylized expressions, the new afflictions of bigotry inevitably dismiss "the other" as "savage terrorists," "Moslem cultists," "Communist puppets" or the like. In expressions even more blatant and sinister, it takes the form of a caricature, i.e. as the greasy Arab with a hooked nose who controls our economic destiny with his greed and petro-dollars; or, similarly, as the Cuban Commie, the fanatic Iranian, the Marxist Nicaraguan, the Puerto Rican Nationalist, the no-good ghetto Black and so on—all of whom are out to destroy the social order that Western civilization wants to etch on this planet.

This is the rub. In the Western psyche, and the American psyche in particular, there are men who inhabit "civilized countries" in the "free world" and men who inhabit, presumably, "uncivilized countries" in other parts of the world. Those mimetic souls in the uncivilized countries, in that unfortunate part of the world that is not free, who toil, in their own unthreatening way, to emulate Western culture and recreate themselves in its image, are the "good guys." By this token, those obstinate peoples going their own route, who are responsive to an indigenous sense of community, national reference and cultural norms are the "bad guys."

This kind of mythology is so handsomely packaged and conveyed by its purveyors that it constitutes a new type of exposition—new in its virtuosity and meaning—to the mass sentiment. Notice how Afghanis fighting against Soviet occupation in their country are "freedom fighters" and Palestinians fighting against Zionist occupation in theirs are "terrorists." No one would dare call fundamentalists in Israel "Jewish fanatics" and "Jewish cultists," but their counterparts in Egypt are called just that. Malcom X, who defied and threatened white supremacy, in symbolism, language and consciousness borrowed from the repertoire of the Afro-American world, was reviled in his time by white society; in contrast, Martin Luther King, who neither defied nor threatened anyone in his aphorismic, rhapsodic utterances about integration, was not.

This is not what one needs to look at—how the master chooses to grace or disgrace those among his subjects with labels. What needs to be looked at is Western society in general, and American society in particular, which believes that it truly is a master, with the population of the Third World its inferiors.

Grammars of human perception do not emerge in a vacuum; they grow in response to the needs of a culture's objective reality. If France is a colonial power, as it was for a time in history—a power that must exploit, pillage and subjugate colonized nations—then it needs to create an intellectual paradigm, such as the mission civilatrice, to justify its acts of exploitation, pillage and subjugation. France was there to "civilize," not to "oppress," peoples considered to be "inferior" to Frenchmen. Similarly, Black Americans remained unfree in the United States for a dozen generations because they were defined as "inferior" in mind and soul and thus could not be trusted to play roles beyond those of farm workers, housekeepers, musicians or athletes."

"If a people is inferior, they should know their place and accept whatever fate is assigned them." If Chileans choose their own leadership, the U.S. sends a team of CIA agents to stabilize the nation (and kill its most prominent members). If the Palestinians state repeatedly, to the point of litany, that the PLO is their chosen representative body, the U.S. and Israel reject this statement and insist on others of their own liking to speak on behalf of Palestinians. If the Iranians, in a revolutionary upheaval thirty years in the making, expel their country's corrupt leader (a leader reinstalled in power by the CIA after he had been rejected by his own people), the U.S. depicts them in such vividly colored, racist mythologies that they are no longer recognizable as the people they are.

The reason French society today reviles the Algerian more than any other "guest worker" is because the French were defeated by Algerians—at the hands of the bicots no less! This is an act that is not easy for the internal psychic economy of a racist culture to absorb, namely, to be dealt a defeat by a community traditionally defined as inferior to it. The racist culture's status, its self-image, its communication about itself, its everyday idiom: are all dislocated. How could an illiterate Algerian bicot, a gook in black pajamas, a Palestinian terrorist with a Kalashnikov, a Zimbabwan nigger with ideas, an Indian wog who goes on salt strikes, respectively kick the civilized French out of Algeria, defeat the mightiest power on earth in Vietnam, prevent the Israeli army from entering Beirut, end white-settler colonialism in Rhodesia, and gain freedom for India?

The literature of power in the last quarter of the twentieth century, in which Third World peoples are reduced to a fragment of their humanity, has a logic all its own. It draws not only on the major body of racist idiom and metaphor that preceded it in the colonial age, but on a new, more subtle syntax of supremacist feelings in society. The recent rise of the extreme right in the U.S. is, in a vital and central way, a racist response—in this case, racists making an inventory of their failures—responding to the increasing boldness of people of color asserting themselves and etching their own reality on the world. The defeats America suffered in Vietnam, in Iran, in Egypt (where its man, Sadat, was offed by "Moslem cultists"), in Nicaragua, in Palestine and elsewhere, are logical forerunners to current jingoism, racist catchwords, epithets and slurs.

In the global dialogue of cultures, America is the arbiter. "That's how it is. That's how it should be." To be obstructed by Frenchmen, Englishmen, Germans, even by Russians, is tolerable. But to be obstructed by inferiors from the Third World is unpardonable.

Indeed, then, though the traditional expressions of the literature of power in European modes of interaction with Third World peoples have declined over the last fifty years, its energies and instigations have neither dispersed nor disappeared; rather, they have animated a new idiom of racism, with its own particular rhetoric or vivid presentation and stylistic liveliness.

Since it is no longer fashionable today to speak of a nigger, a wog, a gook or a bicot, these terms can be subsumed by the term terrorist. Roughly this translates as a kind of collaboration, one might say collusion, between factual material and the literature of power which is eventually spread in an intricate pattern of diffusion to world societies.

In the 1950's the most frightful word in the lexicon of the American social psyche was Communist, or, in the vernacular, "Commie." Though the term carried no racist connotations, it represented in the mind of the average American the most hateful creature on the face of the earth. The term waned, and its power of shaping response atrophied, only when it ceased to serve the interests of objective reality. Today the term terrorist, unlike Communist, evokes not only fantasies about a hateful political being but a hateful human being.

In Israel today, for example, life has become verbalized to a point where aggressions can be siphoned off against Palestinians with no hint of remorse. Israeli soldiers can gang up on a Palestinian child and crush his bones—and go home with elan to their wives and kids at the end of the day—because to them, that child was, literally, a thing. The soldiers had gone through what Franz Fanon called *le process de chosification* The child they victimized was a "chose" (thing), not a human being. In other words, just as the sadist makes an abstraction of the person tortured, so does the Israeli racist, in a frenzied state of mind, see logic in killing, deporting, incarcerating, tormenting and subjugating Palestinians.

The racist instinct is a necessary function of the Israeli's socio-political life. Without it, he would choke under the pressure of historical fact—namely, that not only do Palestinians come from Palestine, but that he has no right to be in their country, tilling their land, living in their homes, inhabiting their cities and suppressing their national identity. The only way he can gainsay that fact, to "unsay" the real world, so to speak, is to deny it. To deny it he has to deny the Palestinians. And that denial, in the end, means the adoption of a perceptual sensibility that "sees" Palestinians as worthless "choses" (things).

Thus, in the U.S., as in Israel (an entity whose political values were formulated by European Zionists at a time when settler colonialism was fashionable), racist images are inevitably programmed into the internal literature of power. Equally inevitable is this literature's appropriation and subornation of terms, values and ideas, reinforcing its selective reading of history. History, after all, is an instrument of the ruling class which can be expected, in any clandestine way possible, to confer meaning on the moment of its own immediacy. The victims of this literature of power do not want to be captive to the judgement of its fictions; but neither can they be expected to allow it to shape the image they carry of historical meaning or of their own individual place in that meaning. This is the problem yet to be resolved.

Fawaz Turki is author of "The Disinherited," "Soul In Exile," as well as a book of poems "Tel Zaatar Was the Hill of Thyme." Former president of the General Union of Palestinian Writers in North America, he represented the Palestinian people at the UNESCO Conference on World Culture in 1982.

Left: Pro-Israeli cartoon portrays Israel as a defender of European and American interest in the third world. Artist: TONY AUTH, Philadelphia Enquirer, Philadelphia, Pennsylvania. Right: Anti-Israeli cartoon portrays Israel as a Nazi Fascist. Artist: RAESIDE, Victoria Times, Victoria, Canada. From the portfolios of the Cartoonist & Writers Syndicate, New York City.

AYATOLLA KHOMEINI

EWK

CORY AQUINO

EWK

MUAMMAR QADDAFI

EWK

JEAN KIRKPATRICK

Oswaldo

MARGARET THATCHER

EWK

LT. COLONEL OLIVER NORTH

Arcadio

YASSIR ARAFAT

Oswaldo

GEORGE BUSH

EWK

Views of the World, CARICATURES: ARCADIO, *La Nacion,* San Jose, Costa Rica; EWK, *Afton Bladet,* Stockholm, Sweden; and OSWALDO. From the portfolios of the Cartoonist & Writers Syndicate, New York City.

IMAGES OF THE FILIPINO IN THE UNITED STATES

BY E. SAN JUAN, JR.

Smiling pink round face, goldrimmed designer spectacles adding intellectual veneer to Corazon Aquino's winsome look as she props her chin, posed proudly to look at readers of Time, Newsweek, Ms., The New York Times: this media fantasy after February 1986 has come to dominate the Western public consciousness today. President Aquino has displaced the legendary Iron Butterfly, Imelda Marcos, in the pantheon of the mass media even as the scandal of billions of dollars looted from the Philippine treasury, the parade of court indictments, under-world shenanigans, etc., continue to define the Filipino stereotype for the U.S. public.

We still see in news items the Filipino running amok in contested villages in the Philippines, the "warm body export" of Filipino workers in the Middle East; Filipinos as "mail order brides," ubiquitous prostitutes around U.S. military bases; hospitality girls in Tokyo, Bangkok, Manila; of late, the Oxford English Dictionary defines "Filipino" as "domestic maids," while in Hong Kong dolls of Filipino women dressed as maids, complete with passport and labor contract, compete as toys in the supermarket.

It was not long ago, just a few years after the U.S. military forces killed over a million revolutionary Filipinos in that little-known episode in U.S. history, the Filipino-American War (1899-1902), that the U.S. public's idea of Filipinos as (in Samuel Gompers' words) "a semi-barbaric population, almost primitive in their habits and customs" found visual confirmation in a scientific/cultural event: the 1903 St. Louis World's Fair where Igorot tribal specimens were displayed. Shades of American Indians in the court of Louis XIV? Not quite. We are in the stage of monopoly capitalism. This now historic exposition may be said to have fleshed, in a scientific/technological spectacle, the rhetoric of McKinley, Lodge, Beveridge and the whole Establishment justifying Anglo-Saxon imperial supremacy.

Over half-a-century of U.S. tutelage has made Filipinos entrenched fanatics of "the American dream of success"; 35,000 Filipinos immigrate to the U.S. annually, accepting low-income jobs even though they are professionals (dentists, engineers, lawyers). This repeats a gesture of sacrifice made by their predecessors. The early immigrants were of course not college graduates; they were recruited peasants hired to work in the sugar plantations of Hawaii, victims of inflated advertisements of wealth supposed to be acquired through honest manual labor. But they learned quickly the reality of U.S. business society. Experiencing the truth of exploitation in a free-enterprise democracy, Filipinos joined the Japanese plantation workers in fierce strikes in the Twenties. The Filipino as violent striker seized the headlines.

During the Depression, Filipinos assumed the role of lynching target, the familiar scapegoat: one instance is the January 1930 killing of two Filipinos and the beating of scores in Watsonville, California, by a mob of 500 white vigilantes. It seemed a repeat of Yankee soldiers conducting systematic massacres of Filipino peasant families in insurgent villages in Samar, Batangas and other provinces in 1899.

One witness of this modern collective ordeal was Carlos Bulosan whose testimony in "America is in the Heart," speaks for all immigrants: "The mockery of it all is that Filipinos are taught to regard Americans as our equals. Adhering to Ameri-

can ideals, living American life, these are contributory to our feelings of equality. The terrible truth in America shatters the Filipino's dreams of fraternity."

Disillusionment, however, gave way to the birth of another ideal. The valiant resistance fought by Filipinos side by side with Americans in Bataan and Corregidor during World War II has inscribed the image of the Filipino freedom-fighter practising racial solidarity in the official annals of U.S.-Philippine relations. MacArthur and Magsaysay are the two symbols linking the two races.

Today it seems like the genealogy of a nostalgia. For indeed that did not change the situation of 9,000 stewards in the U.S. Navy in the 1960s, still called "boys," menial servants who have also joined the kitchen force of the White House and other official residences. In the 1960s, Filipinos as nurses and doctors became visible, with imported nurses acting as scabs and performing work shunned by white Americans and virtually running whole hospitals.

Also in that decade, the case of two Filipina nurses accused of killing patients in a Veterans Hospital in Michigan became a sensational story, projecting Filipinos once more as "devious," "inscrutable," so that in spite of their acquittal, the stigma of wrongdoing still contaminates the milieu of the Filipino worker in the 1960s and 1970s. Meanwhile, the old generation of Filipino farmworkers in California who spearheaded union-organizing in the 1930s and 1940s have finally merged their struggles with the more numerous Chicanos in 1965, with Cesar Chavez eclipsing the figure of Filipino veteran labor-leader Larry Itliong in the formation of the United Farm Workers.

With the exposure of the Marcos regime's corruption and complicity with U.S. reactionary elements in the late 1960s, the Filipino acquired rebel status: political exiles like Benigno Aquino, husband of President Corazon Aquino, and Raul Manglapus, now Secretary of Foreign Affairs, graced the front pages of the metropolitan dailies, side by side with pictures of New People's Army guerillas and Moro freedom-fighters, the latter resurrecting in the popular memory their heroic ancestors who up to the late 1920s defied the Gringo intruders led by Leonard Wood and John Pershing, veterans of the wars to exterminate the American Indians and to pacify the Cuban/Puerto Rican insurgents.

The explosion of February 1986 erased in the public memory any lingering vestiges of the 1903 St. Louis Exposition, the striking militants of the Hawaiian canefields (one of whom returned to lead the Sakdalista rural uprising in the late 1920s), the Filipino guerillas of World War II, replacing them with the scenario of millions of urban workers and middle class Filipinos surrounding tanks and soldiers in the streets of Manila. This February 1986 insurrection, treading closely in the wake of those gory details of Aquino's cadaver bloodying the tarmac of the Manila International Airport, has prompted Filipinos to re-connect once more with their racial origin. I cite a letter from the "Hartford Courant":

> I was born a Filipino. That may seem like an easy statement to make, but even as I write it, I am amazed at the embarrassment I used to feel. Ever since my parents brought me to the United States, I had been ashamed of who I am, and ashamed of my nation . . . .

I was ashamed (as my brother was) of being different. When friends at school said it was disgusting to see my mother serve fish with the head still intact, or for my father to eat rice with his hands, or to learn that stewed dogs and goats were some examples of Filipino delicacies, I took their side. I accused my own of being unsanitary in their eating habits . . . . When Marcos flaunted his tyranny and declared martial law in 1972, . . . I accused Filipinos of lacking the guts to fight for themselves . . . . But everything changed for me when that man (Aquino) I had laughed at landed in my homeland and died on the airport tarmac.

For the first time, I accused myself of not having enough faith in, and hope for, my own people. In the past, I felt that I had no right to be proud of my people. Now, with the cruel Marcos regime tottering, I have finally awakened. Filipinos all over the world need the strength that comes with pride, now more than ever . . . .

Of course it is clear that this Filipina teenager has not heard of the April 1924 strike of 31,000 Filipinos in Hawaii, nor of all the stories of thousands of Filipinos in the farms up to the San Francisco International Hotel saga of resistance in the 1960s which have colored (what an appropriate if paradoxical term) the white American's perception of Filipinos. Yet the past is there for each generation of Filipino-Americans to re-discover and perhaps revitalize, including the fact that as "nonwhites" up to 1946 they could be refused service in restaurants, barbershops, swimming pools, moviehouses, and could not marry white/caucasian women because, as one California State Prosecutor said, Malays are prone to "homicidal mania" called "running amuck." Anti-miscenegation was the name of the game then.

Confusion about the racial category to which Filipinos should be placed has run rampant in the mind of the Anglo ruling elite, from President McKinley up to the ordinary American in the average suburb who could not tell whether the Malay is a Mongolian; whether the Filipino is an African, Chinese, Japanese, or what. Up to now, because of my slit eyes and pug nose, I am still mistaken for being a Japanese or Chinese in school, in the malls, along small-town streets, in church, everywhere. And when I tell the curious observer I am from the Philippines (an original, as they say, born in the islands), indeed, the image of an island in the Caribbean immediately flashes in their minds, expecially because my name (and those of most Filipinos) is Spanish in origin.

If it is of any consolation, one can say that we Filipinos are no longer strangers to U.S. immigration officials. For when the Filipino national hero Jose Rizal arrived in San Francisco in transit to Europe in 1888, he (together with 643 Chinese coolies) was promptly quarantined and fumigated by customs officials on the pretext that they were carriers of typhoid, cholera, leprosy and other "Yellow Perils." Meanwhile, 700 bales of precious Chinese silk were unloaded from the ship without fumigation. In 1908, a Hawaiian farmowner ordered supplies in which he listed after fertilizer the item "Filipinos." Have we come a long way really?

Soon, before the end of this century, there will surely be more than two million Filipinos in the U.S., the fastest growing Asian community centered in the West Coast, in Chicago, New Jersey-New York, and of course Hawaii and Alaska. A volume of family and kin pictures published in 1983 was entitled "Filipinos: Forgotten Asian Americans." Forgotten? Not quite, as long as TV and mass media and everyday gossip feed off the notorious Marcos exploits and the dangers of a Communist takeover in the Philippines.

That historical episode has generated a new semantics of racial categorization which expands it to cover the whole Third World: Marcos joins the ranks of the infamous if legendary Duvaliers, Somozas, Shah of Iran, Noriega and other "not quite civilized" despots to reinforce once again the myth of the West as the virtuous, enlightened homo sapiens civilizing the benighted natives.

Unfortunately the internationally-acclaimed films of the innovative Kidlat Tahimik (Eric de Guia) such as "The Perfumed Nightmare," "Turumba," "Who Invented the Yoyo and the Moon-Buggy?" and others have not succeeded in displacing the Hollywood/Madison Avenue stereotypes of Filipinos as lowly denizens occupying the boundary line between China and Latin America, an enigmatic and heterogenous zone that seems to defy neat racist labelling. Bulosan and other Filipino-American writers remain excluded from the academic textbooks, while the once famous exile Jose Garcia Villa (not to be confused again with Pancho Villa, the Mexican revolutionary) who befriended e.e. cummings and other modernist critics of the hegemonic dispensation, languishes in anonymity in Greenwich Village.

I want to quote a passage from one of Bulosan's letters (written in the 1940s) to recapture and perhaps recuperate the force of the Filipinos' submerged or buried history, a passage which remains emblematic of the way Filipinos (and perhaps other immigrants from the Third World) articulate the moral and ideological core of their predicament as exiles, immigrants, expatriates or refugees—not quite Goethe's "world citizens." Bulosan outlines the germ of his next textual adventure:

I have been wanting to do something of great significance to the future of the islands. I will probably start one of the most important books in my life soon, maybe sometime next week . . . . It concerns racial lies: the relations between Pinoys and white Americans. Here it is: Suddenly in the night a Filipino houseboy kills a friend and in his attempt to escape from the law he stumbles into his dark room and bumps against the wall. When he wakes up he is confronted by a veiled image in the darkness who reveals to him that he has become white. It is true, of course, that he has become a white man. But the image tells him he will remain a white man so long as he will not fall in love with a white woman! And that is the tragedy because he has already fallen in love with a white woman. Get that? So long as he will not fall in love with a white woman! Then, according to the warning of the image, he would become a Filipino again, ugly, illiterate, monster-like, and vicious.

This is a parable, of course, an American parable. Some elements in America gave us a gift of speech, education, money, but they also wanted to take away our heart. They give you money but deny your humanity.

This dilemma has been rehearsed and acted a million times, over and over, in the waking experiences, dreams and nightmares of millions of Blacks, Hispanics, Asians, Native Americans. Repetition breeds truth, as Nietzsche once warned us; but how can we finally break the cycle and construct our identity on the edge of difference? Not to make a mystique of the Other, of difference itself as a virtue, but to identify our desire for recognition via the gaze of the Other?

For the Filipino, I venture to suggest here: the answer is to liberate the homeland from imperial domination and free our minds from the racist manacles forged about a hundred years ago. And still being reforged in the alienating practices of everyday life. This of course is not a Filipino project but that of everyone whose humanity remains locked in the prison of race, gender and class. We may repose our previous questions: Who will rescue the Igorot tribe from that prison of the 1903 St. Louis Exposition? Can the mass media, art and museums as well as our discourse of the tolerant, pluralistic society welcoming "the toiling millions" purge themselves of the poison of racism under the aegis of liberal democracy and free enterprise? That is the urgent question to which we need to address ourselves in the belly of the dying beast.

E. San Juan Jr. is an essayist, author and Professor of Comparative Literature, Department of English at the University of Connecticut.

Above: SICK 'EM. 12 x 19 inches. Artist: J. KEPPLER, *Puck Magazine.*
Below: A FLIMSY BARRIER. 12 x 19 inches. Artist: E.W.B., *The Wasp Magazine.*
From The Balch Institute for Ethnic Studies, Philadelphia.

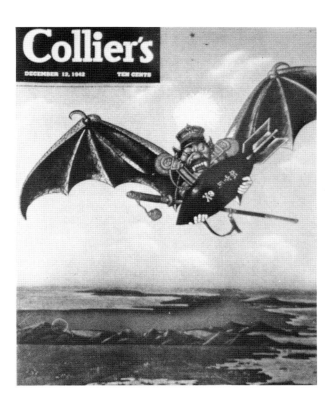

Above left: POSTER. c. 1942, Italy. Anti-semitic poster portraying the stereotyped Jewish Bolshevik. Artist: GINO BOCCASILE.
Above right: POSTER. c. 1942, Italy, Anti-American poster with the theme of 'cultural barbarism'. Artist: GINO BOCCASILE. Like other artists of his time, Boccasile used the black American soldier as an image of cultural barbarism, which he contrasted with the white marble Venus de Milo, an image of European classical purity on which a value of two dollars was placed.
Below left: POSTER. 1937, Germany. For the "Eternal Jew" exhibition. Artist unknown. Below right: MAGAZINE. 1942, U.S.A. Appearing in Collier's Magazine several days after Pearl Harbor, probably did little to arouse American ire. Artist: SZYK.
From the publication: PROPAGANDA, The Art of Persuasion: World War II by Anthony Rhodes. The Wellfleet Press, 1987.

INTEGRATING IN THE COMICS

BY JERRY ROBINSON

The unique blend of disciplines of the comic strip endows it with a visual-verbal experience of remarkable versatility. The comic strip performs one of literature's most important functions—to examine our mores, morals, and illusions. John Bainbridge called the comic strip the most significant body of literature in America. And it was Heywood Broun who credited the comics with constituting the proletarian novels of America.

Cartoons not only reflect American life, but help mold it. William Bolitho described cartoons as the great and indigenous record of life in the United States.

The changing social structure of American society is no better revealed than in the integration of the comics in the 1960's. While there were leading black characters heretofore, notably Lothar in *Mandrake the Magician,* consideration of the Southern newspaper market prevented the syndication of strips with major black characters, except for stereotypes. This was of course also true in other media: TV, films, and advertising. The civil rights movement and the black revolution forced a reevaluation of the role of blacks in the comics, as it did throughout all of society.

In some cases portrayals of blacks were more sympathetic in the early formative days of the comics at the turn of the century, when ethnic humor was less self-conscious, as seen in Outcault's *Lil' Mose* and Kimble's *Blackberries.* Irish, Jewish, and other ethnic humor was prevalent in the first decades. But the role of the black until the sixties was mostly confined to stereotypes in graphics and dialogue, as in McManus' *Hambone & Gravy;* Smokey, Joe Palooka's valet; Mushmouth in *Moon Mullins;* and Asbestos, the stableboy, in *Joe and Asbestos.*

After World War II black action groups such as the NAACP protested the crude portrayals of blacks and their relegation to servile roles of maids, bootblacks, and the like. While the black had not yet achieved his full rights of citizenship, he was no longer an acceptable figure for ridicule. The comic strips that retained black roles abandoned extreme caricature for a more realistic representation. Even Lothar, a sympathetic character and a man of great strength and intelligence, became Mandrake's associate rather than his servant. Ironically, African natives were portrayed more accurately in *Tarzan* by Foster and Hogarth at a time when black Americans were still being given stereotyped treatment. Nonetheless, *Tarzan* drew criticism from UN African delegations for projecting an image of Africa as a continent consisting solely of jungles and uneducated natives.

There followed a period of acute racial sensitivity in the comics. While the stereotypes disappeared, the black could still not be treated with equality and a curious double standard evolved. The special problems were explored in Ponchitta Pierce's article, "What's Not So Funny About the Comics," in *Ebony* magazine in November 1966. Bob Dunn *(They'll Do It Every Time)* was quoted on portraying a black in a bar, "I'm not sure I could let myself go. I'd have to be sure he's sweet and nice and not offensive."

It was felt that the point was not yet reached where the black could laugh at himself. As Al Capp put it, "The day we can draw a Negro, girl or boy, in caricature, or in a funny situation, the civil rights movement will be over." The immediate result was that blacks became less visible on the comic pages, whereas the blacks themselves wanted to get rid of the stereotype and to replace it with roles that reflected their growing participation in society.

In 1961, when *On Stage* featured a black in a major role as a music coach in one episode, four newspapers canceled the strip, three in the South and one in the North. Black officers began to appear in Steve Canyon's Air Force and Kerry Drake's police department.

Until the sixties few black cartoonists achieved national syndication, E. Simms Campbell *(Cuties)* being a notable exception. As did other professions, syndication began to attract the talents of black cartoonists such as Morrie Turner, Brumsic Brandon, Jr., and Ted Shearer.

In 1965 Turner started *Wee Pals,* the first truly integrated strip. The cast includes children of various ethnic backgrounds, and the humor occasionally focuses on race relations. Turner, a former police department clerk in Oakland, California, was inspired by the success of black humorist Dick Gregory. Brumsic Brandon, Jr., introduced *Luther,* another integrated kid strip, in 1968. In 1970 Ted Shearer, a television art director for a major U.S. advertising agency, created *Quincy,* a warmhearted strip (in the *Skippy* tradition) about a nine-year-old black child in a ghetto. To involve the reader with his characters, Shearer includes authentic backgrounds of grimy streets and dilapidated tenements. One poignant strip, for example, has Quincy carrying a glass of water through the street and carefully watering a tiny weed struggling to grow through the cracked pavement. "Gotta let it know someone cares," he soliloquizes.

A stereotyped native chief from an early *Katzenjammer Kids,* the first dialect strip.

Above: The role of the black in early comics as in life, was largely restricted to menial jobs. *Moon Mullins.* ©1926 The Chicago Tribune.
Below: Beetle Baily deals with black aspirations. ©1971. King Features Syndicate, Inc.

Butter & Boop is another strip about a black youngster growing up in the ghetto. Written by Lewis Slaughter and drawn by Ed Carr and Claude Tyler, it began in ten black newspapers in 1969 and was nationally syndicated in 1971. The year 1971 also saw *The Badge Guys* by Chuck Bowen and Ted Schwarz, a humorous police strip with an integrated cast.

In 1968 the first integrated adventure strip with a black co-hero appeared: *Dateline: Danger,* written by John Saunders and illustrated by Alden McWilliams. It featured the reporting team of Danny Raven, a former black football star, and the tall blond Troy Young, who traveled the world pursuing exclusive stories.

The role of blacks in the adventure strip reached its fulfillment with *Friday Foster,* the first black heroine in the strip of the same name. It dealt with the glamorous jet-set world of high fashion and the media jungle. *Foster* was a long-distance collaboration between Jim Lawrence, a veteran adventure strip and science-fiction writer, living in Summit, New Jersey, and Jorge Longaron, an experienced illustrator of juvenile books and comic magazines, who works in Barcelona, Spain. Longaron has a brilliant illustrative style and composed each strip with great technical virtuosity. In spite of his living in Spain, Longaron imbued his strip with a contemporary spirit in his use of authentic new York backgrounds and careful attention to fads and fashions. Integration of the comics suffered a setback in 1973, however, when both *Friday Foster* and *Dateline: Danger* succumbed owing to failing sales.

Curtis, by the talented, young, black cartoonist, Ray Billingsly, was launched in 1988, the only strip with a black hero to be nationally syndicated in two decades.

In the eighty years of comic strips a cycle has almost been completed, where blacks are again featured, although without the earlier stereotypes and the more recent self-consciousness. The comics, along with the rest of the entertainment media, are reaching a greater degree of maturity by appealing to all elements of society and by satirizing and ridiculing the importance of their differences. Of course it would be naive to ignore the fact that the evolution was greatly assisted by the growing market in the black community.

While some deplored the popularization of bigotry and ethnic humor, others welcomed the fact that real problems were at last being dealt with in the comics and on TV. In fact. it became *de rigueur* for strips without black characters to introduce them. In 1968 Franklin, a black youngster, joined the cast of *Peanuts.* In 1970 Lieutenant Flap, a hip black with an Afro and goatee, made his debut in *Beetle Bailey* with the memorable opening line, "How come there's no blacks in this honky outfit?" Three Southern papers refused to run any Lieutenant Flap episodes. even *Stars and Stripes* dropped the strip, but after an overwhelmingly favorable reaction by both black and white readers, it was shortly restored. Walker sees the lieutenant as "just another funny character in my lineup, who will get his lumps and his laughs along with the other dopey denizens of Camp Swampy." Lieutenant Flap may be ushering in a new era of unself-conscious treatment of ethnic characters and a greater sophistication in humor strips.

From: The Comics; An Illustrated History of Comic Strip Art. Published by G.P. Putnam's Sons. Text © Gerry Robinson.

Jerry Robinson is president of the Cartoonist & Writers Syndicate, New York City.

stereotype n. 1: A metal printing plate cast from a matrix that is molded from a raised printing surface, such as type.

STEREOTYPES, OR A PICTURE IS WORTH A THOUSAND LIES

BY JUDITH WILSON

Stereotypes flatten—squash a world of troublesome variety, an extravagant range of depths, substances, textures into smooth, neat, intellectual fast-food orders. In their ability to dull our senses and clog our mental arteries, stereotypes are the antithesis of art. Yet, they are also central to it. Would we recognize a hero in Italian Renaissance sculpture, if he were not equipped with the body of a 19-year-old decathalon winner? Take Manet's *Olympia* or the nude in his *Dejeuner sur l'herbe*. What if she was boney and sunken-eyed like one of Schiele's wraiths? What if she were simply a blonde? In either case, familiar readings of these famous canvases would be disrupted or would at least require adjustment in order to incorporate the signals emitted by emaciation or blondeness as opposed to those transmitted by the trim, but sensuous figures and chestnut hair of Manet's unclothed, mid-19th-century Parisiennes.

To one degree or another, such semantic shifts are tied to a fund of class, gender and ethnic group-specific stereotypes we all continuously imbibe throughout a lifelong process of socialization. Much of the pageant of everyday life would become a forest of indecipherable signs were it not for this convenient cultural shorthand. Our ability to communicate with one another also depends on a certain amount of reduction, generalization, categorization. Otherwise, we would get lost in a maze of particularizing details.

Artists, great or not, if they work figuratively, rely on a store of symbols that includes social types. Art, after all, is a kind of sign-language—exceeding the boundaries of simple one-to-one correspondences, but nonetheless generating "meaning"

along precisely such associative lines. So it is not the business of *typing* that makes some groups "prisoners". The images displayed in this exhibition suggest the problem of ethnic and gender stereotypes has less to do with the limiting properties of group representations than with the relationship between politico-economic power and control of the production/ distribution of social symbols, or put differently, between material and mental domination.

The show's curators have wisely mingled "art" with "non-art" images, reminding us that the social context in which artists operate is partly visual. One need only glance at items like a 19th-century political cartoon depicting Chinese immigrants as "the yellow peril" or contemporary caricatures of figures ranging from Corrie Aquino to Mummar Khadafi to appreciate the extent to which racist, sexist and imperialist icons surround us. Such images are part of the visual context in which artists of a given period live and work.

Ben Sakoguchi's small, corrosively "camp" paintings are based on just these types of mental wallpaper. His subversive redesigning of orange crate labels and movie posters defamiliarizes them, however, making strange the numerous iconographic programmes staring from our grocer's shelves, billboards, even the cereal boxes that greet us each morning. Into the visual cacophony produced by capitalists hawking their wares, Sakoguchi slips tongue-typing elements. For example, a lynched Black man swinging from a tree is part of the label for the artist's "Down Home" brand oranges.

The Pop '60s not withstanding, high art has seldom foregrounded the ethnically "impolite" or impolitic segments of our

Above: Ben Sakoguchi, DOWNHOME, Orange Crate Label Series, Mid 1980's, 10¾ x 11¾ inches, Acrylic on canvas.

mass-reproduced culture. The continued and widespread existence of derogatory images of members of the world's majority cultures is a dirty little secret repressed by many fine artists who exploit pop culture references. During the late '60s and early '70s, however, when a newly emerged Black Consciousness movement enabled Americans of African descent to gaze unflinchingly at painful racial imagery, artists like Betye Saar, Murray DePillars, Joe Overstreet and Raymond Saunders raised the carpet and pointed at the pile of grinning mammy dolls and pancake queens beneath.

Robert Colescott's play with race and gender-based stereotypes began during this period. But unlike the artists mentioned above, Colescott joined a critique of social prejudices with an attack on aesthetic ones. In his 1976 *Natural Rhythm: Thank You Jan Van Eyck,* for example, Colescott wreaked havoc upon the pieties of art history by making the couple in the famous *Arnolfini Wedding Portrait* a light-skinned Black male and his pregnant, dark-skinned bride and substituting a crudely expressionistic painting style for Van Eyck's gleaming, sharp-focused Northern Ranaissance naturalism.

Colescott's recent work dispenses with such canonical references, often replacing them with autobiographical content, but maintains a demystifying posture toward prevalent myths of race and sex. In his preoccupation with the volatile compounds that result from fusing the repressed fantasies of a nation of closet racists and sexists, Colescott is alone among contemporary artists. Only the late Bob Thompson—a late 50s/early 60s figurative expressionist whose work, even at its most sardonic, looks "innocent" in comparison with Colescott's—can be seen as a possible forerunner. *Power of Desire—Desire for Power* (1989) illustrates a staple of post-Bigger Thomas versions of Black male psychology: the notion that White hegemony inflicts Black males with a socio-economically-derived form of penis envy.

Both Robin Michaels and Carrie Mae Weems take on one of the deepest, most treacherous pools of ethnic stereotypes—jokes.

Laughter can be both a vicious weapon and a healing balm. Humor allows us to vent the subconscious' scandalous texts. But it can also veil aggression or mask feelings of vulnerability. In Michaels' 1988 installation *Just Kidding,* racist and sexist jokes about Asian, Black and White women fill the open pages of large books propped in front of photographs of representative females from each group. The offensive texts block our view of the women's faces, suggesting that ethnic jokes and jokes about women obscure their subjects' true identities.

Weems takes a more difficult tack. In a series of uniform-sized photo/text panels, she contrasts particularly foul bits of verbiage and material culture ridiculing Blacks with carefully printed, matter-of-fact-looking images of her subjects. The well-groomed, young Black family that stares back at us above the word "Coons" turns the label sour, shocking, impossible. A handsome youth in profile faces a gorilla who regards us with a scowl. Below, the riddle "What's the cross between a nigger and a monkey?" emits its psychic poison.

Weems has written that she aims for discomfort, that she hopes to jolt unwitting racists into awareness with these works. For this viewer, there is the added virtue that, by withholding commentary—refusing to feed us a closed symbolic message like Michaels'—her pieces stay troubling long after we've assigned them an ideological import. Weems' deadpan presentational style leaves us with a profound sense of the strangeness of ethnic humor, its dependence upon such antithetical impulses as the need to boost one's own dignity by cancelling another's.

Terry Berkowitz confronts us with a politics of *absence* that frequently accompanies advertising. She has coated a rack full of objects white and placed a small television beside them,

with headphones provided to furnish spectators with sound. An unbroken stream of commercials glides by, bearing an almost unbroken string of White faces. There is an equally uninterrupted record of female self-abasement. In order to sell everything from soup to nuts, we see women reduced to ciphers, sex objects, creatures with no desire but to serve others' needs. While people of color have little or no presence in the world of commodity fetishization, White women exist here largely as a void—a ubiquitous presence, they seem absent from their own selves, engaged entirely in suiting themselves to others' purposes.

The inclusion of Tom of Finland's softcore homoerotic drawings reveals another dimension of the stereotype's power. With their chiseled faces and taut bodies, Tom's bikers and leather boys are the male equivalents of Barbie dolls. Their worth defined as the sum of their vital statistics, their ability to delight and/or excite is in direct proportion to the human complexities, flaws, mysteries their cartoon images omit. While such representations smooth and simplify the sometimes perilous terrain of same-sex love, they also reverse traditional masculine roles, giving gay men both the power of pleasure and the power to invest the signs of machismo—motorcycles, military caps, leather jackets—with allegedly subversive, new meaning. Alternatively though, one could argue that in embracing such imagery, gay men remain psycho-sexual prisoners, their libidinal drives steered along conventional, heterosexually-defined paths of dominance and submission.

Finally, different from one another as they are, all of these works share a sense of being outside the arena of conventional image power-brokering. For it is power that assigns ultimate meanings to culture's verbal and visual texts. Thinking about this, I am reminded of a *New York Magazine* article on the late Jean Michel Basquiat. For those sufficiently attuned to artworld minutiae or those who were plugged into the late '70s graffiti/hiphop grapevine, the title "SAMO Is Dead" had a grim poetry.

It was the message Basquiat had left on downtown Manhattan pavements and walls at the time of his transition from street scrawler to professional artist. It was a notice of the dissolution of his partnership with Al Diaz, formerly his collaborator under the SAMO aegis, which had been an acronym for "same old, same old"—street talk for "same old shit" and a phrase immortalized by the proto-rap bards of New York's Latino and Black communities, The Last Poets. But for readers unfamiliar with such history, despite several explanatory paragraphs midway through the story, the title was redolent of an older, much more widely known ethnic sobriquet: Sambo.

I listened to one prominent Black artist vent her rage at this alleged insult and was subsequently startled when a usually savvy Black curator expressed similar outrage. Then it occurred to me that, in a way, they were right. In the U.S., a person of color, even one as famous as Basquiat, ultimately has little or no say over the interpretation of his or her identity. Like women, like gays, we lack the power to name ourselves for the dominant culture.* And as long as this remains true, ethnic, gender and sexual preference stereotypes will retain their corrosive force. As long as this stays true, we're stuck with the same old, same old . . .

---

*In this regard, the recent call for yet another name-change by Black Americans registers as the latest symptom of, rather than soloution to, the problem. During the past thirty-six years, I've called myself "Negro," "Black," or "Afro-American," depending on the decade or occasion. But as far as I know, my doing so has never stopped a racist from calling me "nigger"! I doubt that switching to "African American" will change members of the dominant culture's attitudes or give Blacks greater control over material or cultural production. The term certainly didn't help its 19th-century advocates speed the end of slavery.—JW

Judith Wilson writes on art and currently lives in New York City. She teaches at Syracuse University and is a doctoral candidate in Art History.

PERRY BARD

A stereotype is defined as an "unduly fixed mental impression". The image of the Native American has, in the name of "civilization", been formed through misnomer, misinformation, and misrepresentation. My aim in this piece is to place the origins of this information in a disturbing contemporary context. The information inscribed on the poles dates back to Christopher Columbus. The fact remains that the plastic Indian was made yesterday.   P.B.

Perry Bard, SAVAGE/CIVIL, 1989, 10 x 6 x 4 feet, Mixed media.

TERRY BERKOWITZ

There is a particular aesthetic pushed here in the United States as "the" look to strive for in our society. That aesthetic is white, blue-eyed and blond for the most part with the occasional dark-haired, dark-eyed white beauty or stud as a contrast; it also has an accompanying wealthy lifestyle. This is the role model that appears in the bulk of advertising seen on TV. When the occasional non-white or non-Anglo person is represented on the screen, it is usually as a stereotyped ethnic extreme: the noble Savage, the Geisha girl or Sumo wrestler, the Jewish mother, the athletic or bopping musically adept Black, the mariachi playing Mexican, the carrying-ears-of-corn Indian maiden, the Karate expert or the de's, dem's and dose Mafioso.

The Anglo dream is as much an unrealistic view of our society as the ethnic stereotype. Is it possible that all Anglos have whiter teeth, sweeter breath, cleaner shirts and a better, more valuable life?

IN(DI)VISIBLE attempts to deal with these issues. A small video monitor placed inside a white bread bag plays a collage of image and sound taken from broadcast advertising. The people seen in these commercials are, for the most part, Anglo and white. The "other" people appear either as their ethnic stereotypes or as objects in the background, like a table or chair. Whenever these non-Anglos appear a card comes up that states the % and actual body count of that group in the population according to the 1980 census (the last census for which figures were available). The video is placed on a shelf containing other 'whitewashed' products from Mayonnaise to Uncle Ben's Converted Rice. The viewers listen to the audio through headphones. The audiotrack begins with a foreign voice reciting the Pledge of Allegiance followed by the edited sound of the commercials shown. Over this a voice reads a list of 'white' words: whitewashed, white collar, white man, white cloud, white gloves, white trash, etc. Periodically during the tape, a subliminal message appears for a few frames—it says: ONE NATION. The flashing of this message sets up a rhythm that is meant to hypnotize in a similar manner to what occurs in television advertising itself.   T.B.

Terry Berkowitz, IN(DI)VISIBLE, 1989, 12 x 62 x 16 inches, Mixed media with video.

ROBERT COLESCOTT

ANTON VAN DALEN

Above: Robert Colescott, POWER FOR DESIRE—DESIRE FOR POWER, 1989, 90 x 114 inches, Acrylic on canvas. *Courtesy of the Phyllis Kind Gallery.*
Below: Anton Van Dalen, THE SLAVE SHIP, 1989, 42 x 46 inches, Mixed media.

BING LEE

ROBIN MICHAELS

Above: Bing Lee, COURTESY Of M.O.R.A.L. (Museum of Rejects and Leftovers), 1988, 89 x 59 inches, Mixed media.
Below: Robin Michaels, JUST KIDDING, 1988, 17 x 22 inches each (3 Paintings), Mixed media.

MARTHA ROSLER

BEN SAKOGUCHI

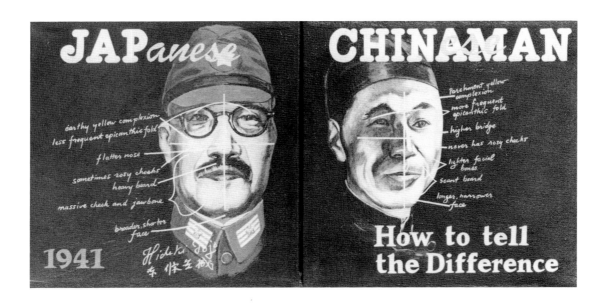

Above: Martha Rosler, PAPER TIGER TV—BORN TO BE SOLD: Martha Rosler Reads the Strange Case of Baby $ M, 1988, Color Videotape: 35 mins. A Paper Tiger TV production.
Below: Ben Sakoguchi, JAPANESE/CHINAMAN, mid 1980s, 10½ x 20½ inches, Acrylic on canvas.

COREEN SIMPSON

Coreen Simpson, JAMIEN, 1984, 60 x 40 inches, Black/white photograph.

LORNA SIMPSON

TOM OF FINLAND

Above: Lorna Simpson, SOUNDS LIKE, 1988, 25 x 22 inches each (3 panels), Black/white photographs with ceramic letters. *Collection of Blanche Gutstein. Courtesy of the Josh Baer Gallery.*
Below: Tom of Finland, Untitled, 1987, 9¾ x 7½ inches, Ink drawing.

CARRIE MAE WEEMS

WHAT'S A CROSS BETWEEN AN APE AND A

NIGGER?

ANSWER: A MENTALLY RETARDED APE

"Stereotypes can assume a life of their own, rooted not in reality but in the mythmaking made necessary by our need to control our world." Sander L. Gilman.

The photographs included here are taken from a larger work which deals exclusively with the stereotyping of Afro-Americans by whites. Black or White, when dealing with the question of racism, we get ta itchin' under our skin, our temperatures rise, our lips quiver; still the major problem of the twentieth century is that of the color line. Personally I'm neurotic, a tad paranoid even, about this color question business. We all are. When confronted (that's what these images do, confront) with questions of racism, we sense our own integrity called into question. The fact is there are more racists disguised as non-racists than you can shake a stick at; so our integrity needs to be called into question, if only to make sure we have any at all. Each of us carries around little packages of consumer racism in the form of neat little characteristics and qualities reserved for specific groups—unlike ourselves—we may encounter along this miserably short course in life. And the unfortunate part of the business is these stereotypes are not harmless expressions, but have real—devastatingly real—effects on the material well-being of those singled out as objects to keep Blacks rooted to work in the past, are the same ones which keep them out of work today.

Folklore taps right at the core of these ugly little prevailing attitudes and is for this reason an excellent socio-psychological barometer. These pieces use folkloric jokes, childhood verses, various mental associations to confront and/or challenge and/or undercut these vogue, but vulgar stereotypes of the Black. For immediacy, the stereotypes are presented photographically in broad exaggeration, and in this way viewers are assisted through the process of self-reflection. C.M.W 1987

Carrie Mae Weems, WHAT'S THE CROSS BETWEEN A NIGGER AND A MONKEY, 1986, 16 x 20 inches each (2 panels), Black/white photographs.

EXHIBITION CHECKLIST

COLLECTIONS:

The Balch Institute for Ethnic Studies, Philadelphia

A FLIMSY BARRIER
12 X 19 inches
From The Wasp Magazine
Artist: E.W.B.

A STATUE FOR OUR HARBOR
AMUSING THE CHILD
12 x 9 inches each
Artist: Keller
From: PUCK Magazine

PAT'S DOUBLE BURDEN
MOVE MONEY WANTED
8 x 9 inches each
Artist: F. Opper
From: PUCK Magazine

SICK 'EM
12 x 19 inches
Artist: J. Keppler
From: PUCK Magazine

UNCLE SAM'S LODGING HOUSE
12 x 19 inches
Artist: J. Keppler
From: PUCK Magazine

Courtesy of The Balch Institute for Ethnic Studies, Philadelphia

The Janette Faulkner Collection of Stereotypes and Caricature of Afro-Americans

ADVERTISING CARD
Cardboard, late 1800s. For Chase and Sanborn Coffee Company.
4⅞ x 6 inches

ASHTRAY
Plastic, 1950s. Nichols Plastic & Engineering Co., U.S.A. 4 x 5 inches

ASHTRAY
Chalk, 1953, Plastic Arts, U.S.A.
4⅞ x 4¼ x 5⅞ inches

BANK
Cast iron, c. 1882. Known as the "Jolly Nigger," this bank was manufactured by the J.C. Stevens Company. The eyes roll when a coin is placed in the mouth and the lever on the shoulder is pressed.
6 x 5½ x 6 inches

CIGAR BOX LABEL
Paper, c. 1910. "Little African, A Dainty Morsel." 10 x 6 inches

CLEANING POWDER
Cardboard. Late 1920s-early 1930s. This depicts "The Gold Dust Twins," an example of using the golliwog/pickaninny image to sell a product. Originally the Fairbanks Brothers used their own portraits on the containers, but sales were slow. They improved when the "Twins" were substituted. The company was later taken over by Lever Brothers.

COMMERCIAL PUNCHBOARD
Paper & wood, 1940s. Used commercially for games of chance. Called "A Darky's Prayer." 16⅛ x 11⅜ x 1 inches.

CUP HOLDER
Chalk, 1930, U.S.A. These are examples of the frequent use of the watermelon as a motif associated with Afro-Americans.
5¼ x 6 x 2 inches.

FIRE CRACKERS
Paper and gunpowder, 1960.
Made in China and Macao.

GOLLIWOG PERFUME BOTTLES
Glass, 1910. These were made by de Vigny Company, France. 6 X 4¼ x 3¼ inches and 3 x 1¾ x 1⅜ inches.

INK BLOTTER
Paper, 1930s. "Satisfaction, Northrup King & Co's Seeds." This was an advertising give-away. Minneapolis & Berkeley, U.S.A. 5⅞ x 3⅝ inches.

MAMMY BANK
Cast iron, c. 1910, U.S.A.
5¾ x 3 x 1¾ inches.

MEMO PAD HOLDER
Plastic, 1950s. The "Mammy Memo Holder" was manufactured in the U.S.A.
10½ x 5¾ x 1⅜ inches.

PHOTOGRAPH
Paper, 1910. "Nigger Head Golf Tees." This is a photograph of a piece formerly in the Janette Faulkner Collection, an excellent example of the theme of violence against blacks masquerading as humor.

PLANTATION ALPHABET
Paper, 1900. The book was published by Ernest Nister and E.P. Dutton Company, New York. Printed in Bavaria.
9¼ x 11¼ inches.

PLATE
Ceramic, early 1940s. "The Coon Chicken Inn" was a chain of restaurants in Oregon, Washington and Utah. 9 inches diameter.

POSTCARD
Paper, 1900. "Buzzard Pete," Detroit Publishing Company. 3½ x 5½ inches.

POSTCARD
Paper, 1900. Flat Finish. "Deed I Dun," American Post Card Company, "Darktown" Series number 76, Ullman Mfg. Co., New York, U.S.A. 3½ x 5⁹⁄₁₆ inches.

POSTCARD
Paper, 1900. Flat Finish. "Expect Us Down Soon," Julius Brent Company, "Comic" Series U.S.A. 3½ x 5½ inches.

POSTCARD
Paper, 1907, Flat Finish. "One of the Good Things Grown in California," Edward H. Mitchell, San Francisco, California.
5⅝ x 3½ inches.

POSTCARD
Embossed paper, 1908. "I'm So Glad this is Leap Year," Leap Year Series.
5½ x 3½ inches.

POSTCARD
Paper, 1914. Flat Finish. The caption reads "Alligator Bait." Cochrane Co., Platka, Florida. 3½ x 5½ inches.

POSTCARD
Paper, 1927. Rag Finish. "Give Us De Rine," Ashville Post Card Company.
3½ x 5½ inches.

POSTCARD
Paper, 1940. Rag Finish. "Honey Come Down," E.C. Krop Company, Milwaukee, Wisconsin, U.S.A. 3½ x 5½ inches.

PRODUCE LABEL
Paper, 1940s. "Coon, Coon Apricots."
4½ x 12 inches.

SALT AND PEPPER SHAKERS
Ceramic, 1950s. These are homemade copies of the "Aunt Jemima and Uncle Mose" premiums offered by the Ralston Purina Company in exchange for boxtops from Aunt Jemima Pancake Mix boxes.
5 x 2½ x 1½ inches.

SOUVENIR SPOON
Sterling silver, 1900s. "Jacksonville, Florida. 5½ x 1³⁄₁₆ inches.

SYRUP LABEL
Tin, 1924. Produced by Robinson Syrup Company, Cairo, Georgia.
7 x 5¾ inches, framed.

TOOTHPASTE
Paper, metal and plastic. Current, manufactured by an English company, a subsidiary of Palmolive Peet, Co., Hawley and Hazel, based in Taiwan. This toothpaste is marketed in Japan, Taiwan and the Middle East.
8 x 1⅞ x 1⅝ inches.

WINDUP TOY
Tin, 1930. "Amos," Louis Marx Company, N.Y. 11½ x 4 x 2¼ inches.

WINDUP TOY
Tin, 1930. "Andy," Louis Marx Company, N.Y. 11¾ x 4 x 2⅞ inches.

Courtesy of the Janette Faulkner Collection of Stereotypes and Caricature of Afro-Americans.

The Cartoonist and Writers' Syndicate Portfolio

POLITICAL CARTOONS
Anti-Israeli cartoon portrays Israel as a Nazi fascist while pro-Israeli cartoon portrays Israel as a defender of European and American interest in the Third World. Both stereotypes exaggerate the truth.

Former: Artist, Raeside
Victoria Times Columnist
Victoria, British Columbia, Canada

Latter: Tony Auth
Philadelphia Inquirer
Philadelphia, Pennsylvania

POLITICAL CARTOONS
These images distort Third World leaders depending on the relationships the "West" currently has with those countries, i.e. Khadafi is portrayed negatively while the image of Corrie Aquino is "cute."

Although a caricature of an individual is not quite the same as an ethnic stereotype it is nevertheless the kind of image-making that generally crates the image of the nation the individual represents.

Top Right: Yasser Arafat by Oswaldo
Top Left: Corrie Aquino by Gallego y Rey
Bottom Left: Fidel Castro by Gallego y Rey
Bottom Right: Mummar Khadafi by EWK
Courtesy of Jerry Robinson of the Cartoonist and Writers' Syndicate Portfolio.

PUBLICATIONS:

MAGAZINE
This caricature, appearing in Collier's Magazine several days after Pearl Harbor, probably did little to arouse American ire.
U.S.A., December 12, 1942
Artist: Arthur Szyk
From the publication PROPAGANDA, The Art of Persuasion: World War II by Anthony Rhodes. The Wellfleet Press 1987.

POSTER
Anti-American poster with the theme of 'cultural barbarism'
Italy c. 1942
Artist: Gino Boccasile
From the publication PROPAGANDA, The Art of Persuasion: World War II by Anthony Rhodes, The Wellfleet Press 1987.
Like other cartoonists of his time, Boccasile used the black American soldier as an image of cultural barbarism, which he contrasted with the white marble Venus de Milo, an image of European classical purity on which a value of two dollars was placed.

POSTER
Anti-Semitic poster portraying the stereotyped Jewish Bolshevik
Italy c. 1942
Artist: Gino Boccasile
From the publication PROPAGANDA, The Art of Persuasion: World War II by Anthony Rhodes, The Wellfleet Press 1987.

POSTER
For "The Eternal Jew" exhibition
Germany 1937
Artist unknown
From the publication PROPAGANDA, The Art of Persuasion: World War II by Anthony Rhodes, The Wellfleet Press 1987.

EXHIBITING ARTISTS:

Perry Bard
Savage/Civil   1989
10 x 6 x 4 feet
Mixed media

Terry Berkowitz
IN(DI)VISIBLE   1989
12 x 62 x 16 inches
Mixed media with video
Video tape: 4½ minutes on continuous loop.

Robert Colescott
Power For Desire—Desire For Power
1989
90 x 114 inches
Acrylic on canvas
Courtesy of the Phyllis Kind Gallery

Bing Lee
Courtesy of M.O.R.A.L.
(Museum of Rejects and Leftovers)   1988
89 x 59 inches
Mixed media

Robin Michaels
Just Kidding   1988
17 x 22 inches each (3 paintings)
Mixed media

Martha Rosler
Paper Tiger TV-
Born To Be Sold
Martha Rosler reads the strange case of Baby $M
1988
Videotape: 35 mins

Ben Sakoguchi
Bananas   mid 1980s
11 x 58 inches
Acrylic on canvas
Down Home
Face To Face
Pachuco
Yellow Peril
Orange crate label series (mid 1980s)
10¾ x 11¾ each
Acrylic on canvas
Japanese/Chinaman   mid 1980s
10½ x 20½ inches
Acrylic on canvas

Coreen Simpson
Doo Rag   1986
60 x 40 inches
Black/White print
Jamien   1984
60 x 40 inches
Black/White print
Richard   1986
60 x 40 inches
Black/White print

Lorna Simpson
Sounds Like   1988
25 x 22 inches each (3 panels)
Collection of Blanche Gutstein
Courtesy of the Josh Baer Gallery

Tom of Finland
Untitled   1980
9½ x 6⅞ inches
Ink drawing

Untitled   1986
9¼ x 6⅛ inches
Ink drawing
Untitled   1987
9¾ x 7½ inches
Ink drawing
Untitled   1987
10 x 8 inches
Ink drawing

Anton Van Dalen
The Slave Ship   1989
42 x 46 inches
Mixed media

Carrie Mae Weems
Ashtray   1988
16 x 20 inches
Black/White photograph
Coons   1988
16 x 20 inches
Black/White photograph
I Wanta Be A White Man . . .   1980
16 x 20 inches
Black/White photograph
Push Cart   1988
16 x 20 inches
Black/White photograph
What You Can't Give a Black Man   1986
16 x 20 inches
Black/White photographs
What's The Cross Between a Nigger and a Monkey   1986
16 x 20 inches each (2 panels)
Black/White photographs

ALTERNATIVE MUSEUM

The Alternative Museum is a non profit museum dedicated to a pluralist approach to the arts and cultural activities of New York on a national and international level.

Our primary concern is to present professional exhibitions and performances with socio-political content while maintaining the highest standards of aesthetics. Particular emphasis is placed on exhibiting the works of mid-career artists.

The Museum welcomes participation in its events from other artists, curators and the community. It is the goal of the Museum to build a true artists museum that is sensitive to both the needs of artists and the public alike.

The Alternative Museum is supported in part by public funds from the National Endowment for the Arts, the New York State Council on the Arts, and the Department of Cultural Affairs, New York City.

The Alternative Museum receives further support for its programs from ABC Inc., American Express Foundation, AT&T Foundation, Edith C. Blum Foundation, Mary Flagler Cary Charitable Trust, Citibank, Consolidated Edison Company, The Cricket Foundation, Department of Cultural Affairs, City of New York, The Jerome Foundation, Philip Morris Companies Inc., The Rockefeller Foundation, The Weatherhead Foundation, and the Associates of the Alternative Museum.

Design & Production,
Janice Rooney

Printing,
Athens Printing Company
New York City

4440

ALTERNATIVE MUSEUM   ISBN 932075-24-X